A Different Land

Palewell Press

A Different Land

Poems – Frank McMahon

A Different Land
First edition 2022 from Palewell Press,
www.palewellpress.co.uk
Printed and bound in the UK

ISBN 978-1-911587-65-1

All Rights Reserved. Copyright ©2022 Frank McMahon. Except for reviewers who may quote brief passages in a review, no part of this publication may be reproduced or transmitted in any form or by any means, without permission in writing from the author. The right of Frank McMahon to be identified as the author of this work has been asserted by him in accordance with the Copyright, Designs and Patents Act 1988

The cover design is Copyright© 2022 Camilla Reeve
The cover image of Nine Standards Rigg in The Pennines is Copyright 2022 Frank McMahon
The photo of Frank McMahon on the back cover is Copyright ©2022 Frank McMahon

A CIP catalogue record for this title is available from the British Library.

Acknowledgements

Poems have been published in Erbacce, The Steel Jackdaw, Trouvaille Review, The Cannon's Mouth, Galway Review, Makarelle, Beecraft, Sarasvati, Off the Wall and Dialect Writers Anthologies.

"The Stag" has been accepted for the anthology, For the Silent. to be published by Indigo Dreams Press.

Dedication

These poems are dedicated to my family:
Dorothy
Anna and Jonathan
Mark and Ione
Sam, Tom and Dora
Orla, Briony and Aggie

And with very special thanks to
Anna Saunders
Somewhere Else Writers, Wordbrew
and DialectWriters

Contents

THIS LAND CAN TAKE YOU DOWN	1
A Different Land	2
The Stag	4
Breaking New Trails	5
Pilgrim Track to Mont St Michel	6
Long road home	8
FOR THIS IS POLICY	9
The Caves of Matera	10
The Sanatorium	11
I hear those voices which will not be drowned*	12
Preparation for a Process	14
The Ferry	16
THEATRE OF AIR BLOOMS	17
Held	18
Sixteen Swans	19
Blackbird	20
Citrus	21
Limestone Bells	22
Sonata	23
Tete-A-Tete	25
Rose Garden	26
Tracking Back	27
I contemplate	30
AND WHAT SHALL WE NOT TALK ABOUT?	31
The Christmas Menu	32
Threads	33
Weight	34
Beyond the Afterlife	36
Fingerprints	39
Becoming	40
Restless	42

LOVE IS LOVE IS LOVE 45
    Passajes 46
    Love Might 48
    A fox 49
    The Gift 50
    Lock and Key 51
    Love is love is love is love… 55
    Du Fu Comes to Our Home 56

Frank McMahon– Biography 58

THIS LAND CAN TAKE YOU DOWN

A Different Land

Nine Standards Rigg. From distance
nine enormous teats of a beast inverted,
suckling the clouds. Waymarks to a no man's land.

Memorial walk. Uphill, one last stone wall,
tufts of scrawny grass, meadow pipits' rapid calls
dissolving. Jet black path, millstone scatter.
A distant curlew.

Nine cairns standing north to south on England's spine.
If four of us stood fingertip to fingertip
we might surround the girth;
if you stood on my shoulders you might just
                                      touch the top.

This is borderland where west meets east.
There is no simple passage from this portal.

This land has defined its intrinsic purpose.
It offers no negotiation. A plough would drown
in this living graveyard growing with its dead.
Motherlode, dreich wilderness of treasures,
water-breathing alveoli
ten thousand years of rain
swelling sphagnum's membranes, held and routed
to nourish becks and rivers. A carbon sink,
this ground sequesters our excess.

It stretches out ahead, a vast dun pelt
raddled with pitch-black veins.
It will permit your crossing, absorb
the slap and slubber of your boots,
will in time repair itself, swallow your footprints.
This land commands respect.

Ravens' land, acidic, this sponge has room for bodies
slithering over slabby earth, confused
in thickening mizzle, sucked into a grough
or slack, pressed down by heavy clouds.
Shouts do not carry here.
Face and hands preserved emerge
from Goretex, compass fouled and rusted,
in clotted rucksack a half-eaten lunch.

Do not cross this place at dusk.
Nightmares brew in brackish pools,
bog monsters sheep-devouring, cloaked in sedge, rise
from quags and long abandoned folds.
Do not show a light or breathe too loud.
Hurry slowly.
This land can take you down like grief.

The Stag

A raven's flight splits the rising sun.
A curlew sings.

Their scent comes through cracks in the sky.
The stag turns his head searching for direction
in the compass of his gaze,
moves beyond sight to lower ground
of streams and quags. He turns.

The crest of the hill brims with silent hounds.
Their breath steams, tongues wash the air.

He stumbles, moving uphill
to find the ridge, bellows as if in rut.
The morning throbs with fear and lust.

Too many to resist. Plangent,
a long bass note echoes
in the chamber of his throat.

Masked riders lead the hounds away.
An entry in the hunting book.
On grass and ling
a darkening smear of blood.

Breaking New Trails

Stretching out an arm you saved a colleague's life,
pulling him back from the edge of the cliff.
"So what?" you said later.

In the heated run of business you were never too pressed
to grasp the rough-edged arguments and dovetail
to a compromise. And you had strength

to work across the grain, running your plane
smoothly through the knots, riding the warp
with a generous hand.

You returned from Corsica renewed, drew for us
flower-rich meadows, hours of hard climbing,
pure air and sunlight.
                Then without warning you broke new trail,
left us to try to follow
the maps you left behind.

Pilgrim Track to Mont St Michel

Here,
tides can outrun the swiftest runner in this vast bay
scalloped between dune and salt marsh. Here
wind and light and water rule.
The guide announces "pieds nus",
not even sandals but we accede, secular itinerants,
subscribed to be guided to the Mount and home again.

In his knowledge and our fitness we place our trust
through scattered pebbles, empty mussel shells, hard-ribbed
undulations and where
the soaked sand demands the deliberate placing and retraction
of our feet
                plunge and lift   plunge and lift
until the thigh-deep crossing of the river and reaching the bank
the Mount is clear, stone and glass, layer on layer until the spire
challenging the sky.

We hope he can read the weather's alterations, shifts of tides
and unexpected surges;
stories of pilgrims carried away, in too much haste, gambled on
the light prevailing,
the roar of eternity in their ears.

Look seawards, figures emerge.
Horizon dances a wall of haze and shimmer, permeable border
between two different worlds.

Would this be a truer test of faith to walk towards it, hesitant
deliberate, to walk, knowing what lies beyond it is the sea
but never knowing
                until you enter
                                  how you will be received?

Long road home

It was as I remembered it, the long, rough track
and the plain squat house.
Gone my uncle loading churns onto the cart
and the heavy horse patient in her traces,
gone the hens squabbling around my aunt
as they hunted for the broadcast grain.

I waited, turned and was greeted by a shout,
"I know who you are!" A stranger pulling my face
from the leaves of the family tree.
He urges his herd of cows through the gate
and invites me back to his home, explains
it was he who had taken on this farm.

We sit around the table in the long, white-washed,
single-storey house, sip tea, swap news,
made welcome but chided in equal measure.
My brothers had kept in touch, honouring this house
as the new, authentic family locus.
But I had been neglectful, had somehow failed
to understand my obligations,
to comprehend the loss of names and genes,
sisters all, to make new lives and homes abroad.

And so I sat, civil, lovingly discomforted
until I'd paid sufficient dues, could rise,
give thanks and leave, powerless
to replace the growing emptiness
in school and shop and church
and round this hearth.

FOR THIS IS POLICY

The Caves of Matera

Outside a piper played
while the children went into the mountain,
their parents too.
There was nowhere else for them to go
and what could be imagined
had best remain unseen.

And the mountain needed to be hollowed
as more children went inside,
in two's and three's at twilight.
Tunnels, galleries, caves;
daily ordure taken out with the spoil
from chiselling and digging,
door-frames and lintels made from children's bones,
flesh-shadows imprinted on the walls,
a gallery of the dead..

Inside the mountain, voices were lost
in the cracks of granite, no words
escaped on the mountain's springs;
hunger knocked at every make-shift door
but the piper was never sent
to bring the children out.

The Sanatorium

Pastel-tinted walls, pristine surfaces,
air filtered to exclude external contagion,
clear views from well-positioned windows,
prescribed diets glowing in bowls
an exercise regime scrupulously followed.

This is a place of superior knowledge
which knows how to diagnose every condition;
we can draw upon the history of dangerous pathologies,
especially those diseases of the mind
which lead to bodily disorder.
Here we provide smiling, firm instruction
to work towards our goal,
the search for harmonious living.

In time the yellow smog and sandstorms will abate,
(a permitted consequence of progress).
Here your mind can dissociate and consider
from this mountain top the future. Of course
some pathogens require more rigour
and persistence to eliminate.
Our arc of history tends towards perfection
where you and they and we are all in step.
We have taken on the burden of your doubts
so you may observe
how clear the dawn and the lotus stirring with its light.

I hear those voices which will not be drowned*

The sea keeps a log
of journeys, sinkings,
rescued, drowned;
somewhere in its flux
are particles of vowels,
long, clogged cries
which stripe the underside of waves,
noises dispersed
which salt will preserve.

Exhausted by flight
harrowed by hope

who heard what passed
from lip to ear
as they climbed aboard
to hazard all
when turning back
was hazard?

What extra costs do they carry
in their muted carapace
those who survived?
What pictures to erase
before they die?
I hear the shingle groan;
shrieks like knives on glass
thresh and retch
calls   falling   failing   fading
shouts
        tss   tss
                shhh   shh   sh.

I hear the shingle utter
its indictment.

*Peter Grimes by Benjamin Britten.

Preparation for a Process

What you have done so far
are you willing to go beyond what you have escaped?
Why is not my right to ask so,
I speculate from the dense catalogue of crimes
(imprisonment, spilled blood of family, burnings,
death march in the night)
we must stop there but there is never where it ends
and how you edged your way (the furtive escape,
miles with blistered bloody feet,
dark corners of fields or public squares)
again I speculate:
your via dolorosa is unique
and how you crossed to reach this shore, yes,
you'll need to explain how
you came (endless trains, in leaking boat,
concealed in a lorry or container); and why
you never made the application instead of setting out
(they'll say there is a process and a form)
why you didn't stop before (oh, they'll say,
so many countries before, so many
opportunities before today)
            to say the words you're about to utter soon.

It's all POLICY from where you fled, through all those borders,
to where you are now; it's all POLICY, voices shouting
"send them back" and THEY have to be listened to.
You may have heard them already, if not, inure yourself.
There are questions before the questions and before them all:
squalid barracks or fetid rooms
a constant insufficiency
shouts and murmurs in the dark, dimmed eyes, the long gaze
at the floor as if an ant is making its purposeful way;

and the cardinal virtues for survivors:
courage-   an orchid in a long dry season
patience-   counting grains of sand at night
hope-   the ebb and flow of irregular tides
grief-   a wolf at the door
memory-   what you pray to forget.

You must remember these and then forget them
when the moment comes, when the eyes
and the voices give no sign of hope
when your mind is a swarm of mosquitoes
you must have clarity
speak with a tongue like tempered steel
prepare to repeat repeat repeat
and wait wait wait keeping a chain on your fears
for this is POLICY as well.

The Ferry

departs, decks and cabins empty. We turn inland,
no goods or passengers disembarked. This for a month or more
as we gather every Friday on the jetty and begin slowly
to parcel out bewilderment. 'Phones no longer work,
no other way to reach beyond our shores.

We meet in Autumn's fading days to forage
for potatoes in the furrows, root like pigs
for windfall fruit, jostle at the farm
for dwindling milk and cheese.
Consideration shrivels.

The ferry comes, turns in the harbour;
once a member of the crew waved,
was swiftly pulled inside as the ferry left.
Yet still we come each week,
huddle against the northern gales,
discuss the burial of the dead, remedies for the sick,
too weak to row and trail a net for passing fish.
Each time we shout, wave lists of necessary items, debate
rowing out to try and board.

The ferry comes and leaves, wake dissolving slowly,
lights blurring in the fog, each ten seconds the klaxon
fainter and fainter.

THEATRE OF AIR BLOOMS

Held

Pulse
                Pulse
                              Pulse
                                              Pulse
salt-shift   water- shift
retreating susurration.
Theatre of air blooms with sea's exhalation
so-sure   so-sure   so-sure   so-sure.

From a veiled bank of sand
Will-will-will-will-will-will
                        ripples across placid water

pulse
          pulse
                    pulse
                              pulse
          rapt   rooted

Held   Held   Held.

Sixteen Swans

After Sibelius 5th Symphony.

When they arrived the water parted like furrowed hail,
like snow blown through open windows,
like the manuscripts strewn across his study floor,
like music, sounds in freefall, too many to gather
and arrange on parallel lines, a man
trying to capture feathers in a gale,
lungs at the point of bursting.

His daughter pointed them out, moving
demurely like ladies at a soiree,
discreetly straightening a ruffled skirt, silent
as if waiting for the string quartet to play.

In the morning they had gone. Commanding solitude,
he sat, notes churning, day after day,
watching until the swans returned,
their steady unhurried wing-beats,
tireless regular undulations, over and over,
circling patiently, choosing the place, the angle of descent.

His pulse slowed to their rhythm, felt it imprint within.
And as they broke the water's surface, the scattered spray
fell and rose, fell and rose, fell and rose, arranged itself.

Blackbird

He's there again on the apex of the gable,
telling the world he's got the title deeds
to number 14. There's a boundary, not marked
on any map but he knows where it is,
so stay outside. Unless of course you're a female
looking to share a very des.res. And raise a brood.

Was there ever a warning sign as musical as this?
Not the baritone drone of the collar dove
or the obbligato chatter of the sparrow's octet,
not even the starling's jazzy chuckling
somewhere between a sax and clarinet.

No, none of these but the fluted mastery
of notes and scales, the end stops of our waking day
as he rings down the dark-blue curtains of the sky
and echoes curl inside the silent leaves.

Citrus

Beads of rain are the brightest light
this morning, replenishing the winter's soils.
Dark seems to fall each dawn
and seep from the radio's news,
install itself on the breakfast table.

Arancia, naranja. Slightly ruckled peel
gleams in my hand like a small star
descended or tiny segment of the sun
which flared and journeyed overnight.
Genius of grafted rootstock brought
on a westward arc.

                Something like
a serious conversation, this fruit requires
enquiry, sight and touch and scent,
a subtle knife to test what it contends,
shave peel, extraneous pith, then slice,
excising pips, preserving
the intensity of flesh and juice.

Arancia, naranja: perhaps a journey
into love where you trust the promise
will always be upheld, working, working
to its bitter-sweet heart, waking
each day to the gift of its light

Limestone Bells

Necessity requires their resurrection,
shaped to repair a crumbling wall,
this time a different mode of kinship
beneath this ragged canopy of trees.

A warm sea washed here once,
replete with tidal thresh and murmur,
muffled volcanic thunder, tectonic grind
as the stone was born, carapace on carapace.

Rippling through autumn's cloisters
and the whispered chants of descending leaves,
to the strikes of the mason's hammer
the stones are singing.

Sonata

After Beethoven opus 109

1.

It's as if someone has just turned up the volume
while I am sitting at a table in a square
half-watching the sparrows, sipping a cafe corretto
when voices arrive from my left, sit down nearby
and without meaning to I start to ride on their rhythms,
catching the occasional word, going
with the undulations; as if their conversation
was always there, something like
the expanding universe or I'm on an island mid-stream.
And I wonder how he heard it,
where it had lived
before he wrote it down,
how it could grow out of silence.

2.

An argument breaks out.
The square becomes a stage
and we an involuntary audience.
The air is brusque and bruised,
laced with vinegar and bile;
the protagonist's ears are anvils.
Discord and departure.
Nothing is resolved.

/**continued**

3.

In the hollow of the silence
a word, a phrase, tentative,
as if they're sampling silk or lace
but distracted by some other thoughts
like a task to be done
but half-remembered
or a face they thought they knew
crossing the sunlit piazza;
words, phrases, piano, because the morning's skin
requires balm and soothing fingers to apply,
easing the ache,
molto cantabile, molto cantabile

Tete-A-Tete

Almost an act of faith, planting out
those bulbs before the winter's frosts, all
self-contained like monks in contemplation, hooded
in winter's cowl. Sunk deep enough to hold
their memory and purpose, shallow enough to let
them sense their moment of release.

As we sit, converse and fret,
look along the empty roads,
before us Tete-a Tete quietly building
the season's cloisters, gilding the columns so brightly
we have to shield our eyes.

Rose Garden

In shade from the hot Spring sun, I try
to count the colours round these walls
but lose myself in the tumbling blooms.

We're under the starlings' flight-path,
left to right then left again, roof ridges as
terminals, a chaffling conference then lift-off.
Way above, the muted one-tone roar of a jumbo-jet,
rare visitor this spring, trailing its smoke
through the cerulean dazzle of a cleaner sky.

Look down and round to light-buttered yellow,
white-pink and white and crimson, dark as plasma,
your gift of thorn and bud to grace
these all-enclosing walls.

Tracking Back

Glottal stops under the dockers' umbrella,
snotty adenoids dispensing scally wit,
claw-hammer life, wrenching a living

from the riverside, humour salving
the salted wounds. The river shrugged its tides
back and forth, shucked departing ships

across the globe, our dad returning with exotic gifts,
fire crackers, sugar cane. Oil strikes
under the sand, our castles black as slate,

effluent round our ankles as the Liver Bird
looked down. Skin blistered, dabbed with cold
tea, tannin on tan and freckles, late night

wincing, doubled with doses of syrup of figs.
Cobblestone cricket between the ennog's walls,
impromptu plays with neighbourhood kids,

the scar still on my finger where the penknife
cut. Our own estate, this park, Paxton's gift,
roaming wild amongst the cultivated shrubs,

on full alert for the uniformed keepers.
Snow fall, ice leaves inside the window pane,
paraffin-scented bedroom, fire banked

with nutty slack. Chilled fingers scribbling
numbers, formulae, sines and cosines
eels beyond grasping, acalculia,

/continued

steer from Pythagoras to Homer and beyond.
Football and fights in the vestry,
angelic faces altar-wise. African

missions, stations of the cross,
sado-masochistic hagiography,
blood and gall incubus of guilt,

thurifer swinging, chanting repetition.
Retreat to consider eternity; beach,
bird, grains of sand, quicksands

of eschatology, feet mired in fear
and shame. Step backwards, turn aside,
find a reef of disbelieving, move

to your moment of quiet rebellion.
Words will fall and fall.
Taught to think and question, exhorted

to accept unblinkingly the faith,
something had to give. And did.

Wheat in a gale, the Kop surges
and sways, passion jammed shoulder
to shoulder, raw, red roar.

A city in slow decline but high
on its otherness. "This is us!
and do not try to fuck us over!"

We lived across the water but we could
feel the pulse, the Mersey Beat,
stood and shouted "Yes!"

Roam, run wild in the hills and woods.
And then we had to go, go south
then I, west to a strange, complacent place,

where, quiet and confused at first, I found
the voice, my voice, shouting my anger
at the world's wrongs. It never left,
drove me on to try to change the grain.

I contemplate

water, the quiet stream
falling along the shallow weir, saturated sky,
rain-drops loosely-laced across grass,
cattle feeding at the hay-stall.

I contemplate water; under grey light
birds of common plumage excavate
autumn's sodden leaves; yellow fluffs
of lichen gleam dim in thorn and ash.

I contemplate water always evicting itself:
distant, insistent sound of traffic,
fleched flight of geese migrating south,
the journeys of the homeless and displaced.

I contemplate water, what it brings
and what it takes away, where it never goes
or is diverted for advantage.

I dream another landscape,
a shared and common well.

AND WHAT SHALL WE NOT TALK ABOUT?

The Christmas Menu

RAF Airbase, Italy, 1944

As if we are not here
in order to forget what brought us here,
little on these tables grown in this land
except the crimson wine bubbling in our mugs;

so that, as if, we can pretend
to be at home, hats, streamers, turkey,
the pudding flamed.

And what shall we not talk about?
Deep in our cups remember the silent rule,
names no longer rostered, griefs deferred,
death's impossibility in the ranks of the young.

And yet and yet
where would we rather be but here
where our laughter is our bond
our recklessness our refuge
our fear dissolving swiftly in this wine.

Tomorrow we will think about tomorrow,
grateful for today.

Threads

He sits in the silence
of the stricken house.
The telephone rings unanswered.
Light intrudes through half-drawn curtains.

Slowly he rises, trails a finger
through accumulated dust,
a photograph, a wedding
where the first hopeful threads were spun.

Their home, his home now,
is a boat unmoored.
The severed cordage of their years
hangs,
throbs.

Weight

The knee on the throat
emphatically placed,
history's weight
in the marrow of the bone,
peine forte et dure.

Like phosphorus, a moment breaks
and the trail of light
arcs back, seconds, centuries,
to ships, dark holds crammed
with measured flesh, cargo degrading,
numbers of deaths redacted,
an attritional expense.

Family history can offer some purchase
on injustice: flight from famine,
begging a boat to another shore;
Black and Tans, civil war,
no Blacks or Irish here.

Whiteness is a passport from the past,
provides a place of watchful safety,
an escape route for descendants.

Empires live beyond their graves
in myths and statutes, whips replaced
by deadlier force,
manoeuverings, suppressions.

The knee
upon
the
throat
hovers like the ghost
of an unchained hound.

Beyond the Afterlife

Hot, frayed, a public square, roads seven or eight
begin or end there, arteries, each trodden by a marching band,
determined footsteps, brass and timpani and flutes,
their anthems swelling louder, all with a different score;
and the drums thump as they seek the dominant position,
face off against the rest, the notes in combat
ragged   louder   louder
until the pigeons flee the discord.

Black
the print on the Constitution's page,
"three fifths of a human being."
The merits (or otherwise) of an unwritten constitution
permit ancestral text to be denied but it creeps,
through gaps and open windows,
creeps and settles like unpaid bills;
any finger can trace a line to the unexamined archive,
to the cellar where what was filtered out escapes
from the carefully edited page and the wax-sealed box,
the secrets in the corners of white spaces.

Union jacks were lowered long ago, lines of mourners
dwindled, medals and coins with Imperial heads
twitch in boxes of family heirlooms.

Empires live beyond their graves and our hearse lurches on;
a new fleet sails to the East questing for the past while
statues are toppled from quayside and plinth.
A pyramid of exotic fruit teeters
topples
as the orator tugs at the base, selects,
cuts the flesh, reveals the liquefaction.

To exhume the past when the present is so perplexing
(starvation, plague, the world facing death
by fire or water_____)
may seem indulgent to those who are not "other."
What would WE say if.....................?
When he opened the lid of the box a swarm,
mosquitoes, hurled themselves   outwards
as they danced and bit,
how did they find their way in there?
or were they always present?

Empire, paradigm of wealth extraction,
gradient of lesser regard:
disposable labour, indentured, trafficked women, slaves
and what others learned from us, the Untermensch;
the lessons acquired from the games of maximising profit
are passed from winner to winner, laundering gains off-shore.
Empires live in the super-yacht
in the untold story of the stately home.

/**continued**

The past is a mirror to ourselves. In its reflection
we can't reshape our crooked timber but oh!
the lens reveals   and yes!
it was a shock, no other word will do
to see the soot and accumulated grime distorting,
ascribing a lesser value.   I was misled, no!
I had failed to question the version accepted
or shall we say   authorised?

And the hearse lurched on, leaking an incontinent bacillus;
so the fever rose
notices on windows
firebombs and faeces
people dragged to the execution ground
the weight on the throat emphatically placed
and always the chorus of casual comments
threat abuse from deep in the forest
fever's embers stoked for advantage
the descant of coded comment,
and when speech is required   their silence.

I imagine a future as something like,
when coming back from a country walk
past the first houses a flute, someone practicing a melody
all clear and fine until the fingers stumble   some false notes
discords, a pause then a second, third closer to the heart of it
until the shadows vanish and the places where we live
are no longer haunted.

Fingerprints

With a touch, finger-light, breath
of water-drop falling past a leaf,
so light you nearly miss it, another,
more, irregular repetitions
until a scratch a hangnail's jag; voices voices voices
as if the last train has just gone and they've nowhere else to go.

People
falling over and it's time,
urgent time to stop and hold this finger
examine its heat   whorls and circles,
useless as the clues are deep inside the bloodstream.

Out there   outside
more fingers and thumbs hands claws talons   inserting
and blood
windpipes choking like a drain
and the smack of breathlessness breathlessness

Out there   outside
fingers on the window etching graphs, obituaries
and the curtains will not close;
waxing moon, Venus standing East in retreating light
bats cleansing the air of insects
whirling
rapacious circles   night
death's fingerprint.

Becoming

I stuff ice into my nostrils
to stop the bleeding
ram stones into my ears
to stop the noise.

Raised unfettled
in a breaker's yard
less than the sum
of my meagre parts
deducted ineluctably,
kettled to this corner
of a leaking shed;
rust   dust
doomed light on the treadmill.
And did those feet?

"Sorry, spider, did I disturb you?"

Heartbeat, heartbeat, heartbeat
why can't I wish myself unborn?
Why does life insist
when the monster lurks behind?

Cogito   ergo   sum-thing.
I will open my door today.
And then?

Agit-bubble   steam   ice
bleb   graupel-lashed

water must find a way,
whatever
water will find its way.

Restless

We are restless.
You always knew that, learned
about springs and neaps, storm surges.
We always draw you back
to the edge of sand or shingle,
tentative paddlers or full immersion,
testing yourself against the potential
of our power, perhaps paying homage
to the source of your origins:
amoeba, fungi, lungs and wings.

Remember, we always welcomed those
who had a more serious purpose,
mariners and fishermen sharing our largesse.

We are restless now
in a different way;
some of us are choking
as you force-feed sludge and poison;
the home we offer others is dying
as you scavenge, slaughter tomorrow's harvest.

What we shared with cloud and rain,
what you took as given, take what is changing now
as friendly warnings
and not some acts of random malice.
At least not yet.

We increase as you melt
our frozen stores. Where, we ask,
can we go, certainly no deeper.
Out of our waters it rose
this land you rule, incontinent warlords.

We are rising,
coming to reclaim,
not, you might think, in vengeance
but to save ourselves

and perhaps in time save you.

LOVE IS LOVE IS LOVE

Passajes

Foreign countries then: consonants percussive
splintering the air, the long throb of diphthongs
breathed con passion. And we, lost
amongst those sounds, working our language
in the times when our bodies would fall mute.

Heat of night and day. Seeking the cool
Atlantic waves. Everywhere the Guardia Civil,
stubbled jowls and hostile stares, sub-machine gun
hanging from the shoulder, the old dictator's
shadow cowering the land.

A man skins a bull, blood spills,
children swim in the reddening sea.
We drive on cobbles underneath dark archways;
old men in berets fade into the walls.

Crisp white wine, slow lunch as a theatre
unfolds, hands stretched out and clasped,
flamboyant scarves, cheek to cheek
embraces, a long formal dance between the tables
as we watch discreetly in Anglo-Saxon rectitude.

The geography of love, contours of word
and gesture, formed by the wash of history,
familial residue of silt and stone.
The language of love bursting to escape the lexicons
inherited: constraint, sub-text, whispers.

Res publica: new voices in the forum,
argument and clamour, harmony and stasis,
patterns improvised, unchartable.

Love Might

arrive with a thunderclap
or come as an unexpected parcel, bound
with many strands of string; close-tied
knots to be teased apart by patient,
nimble fingers.
                      Bright silver wrapping
to remove with care. Open the lid
of the box and peer inside to see
a door which opens outwards.

Walk through and look around.
The door closes softly with a click
and disappears.

A fox

crept into my sleep. The thin mesh fence
trembled as his snout searched for gaps;
a grandchild shivered with fever,
sweated, pain pushed across his borders.

Front paws began to scratch and dig;
how deep had I set this barrier,
how firm the posts and staples? Friends
growing distant, encircled by wilder,

self-created beasts, news from their outside world
tipped with curare as we, unsure,
watched a flat, calm sea,
shielding our eyes from the troubled light.

Musky breath, eyes intense, probing still,
walking a warder's circuit of the wired enclosure
as sea-fretted drifts of music lingered
from the day: Mahler, "what the flowers tell me".

Too active this dance for 2 a.m. but
the brambles by the river promised fruit
and the last squash were gathered in.
The fox indicated, look, look

at who is beside you, sleeping;
remember your shared and tranquil days,
the liquidambar leaves a garnet blaze
and Mahler again, "what love tells me."

Each night now the fox revisits.

The Gift

At the midsummer's zenith
amber light is harvested and stored,
springtime's gathered rainbows spun and melded
into lustrous bronze in the prism of the jar.

The lid, unsealed, releases
a compressed compendium of scents;
lavender and clover fill the room.

Each spoon dipped lifts a viscous
log of journeys, a manifest
of pollen-heavy loads.

Savour slowly,
step outside and listen, listen
as summer's work continues.

Lock and Key

1.

The lovers dance in a cone of light,
enclosed, an embryo,
dance as if no one else is there
then move, coming closer
beneath a sky which is spawning stars
and the slick pavement a galaxy
lighting their way to the bridge
which groans with the weight of padlocks.

Can love be such a burden?

2.

What they hold suggests some kind of closure
when it's only the beginning.
Better accept that it's all negotiation
even in these sweet impulsive moments.
They aren't the only couple closing the shackle,
turning the key, which they drop conjointly,
inaudibly, as we speculate on what
is being locked in, locked out.Or both.
The bridge has become a museum
of passionate pledges, anonymous.

                                            /continued

3.

If these are moments where promise leads
to wedlock or something like,
to the working out of intentions
trial and negotiation
where the sum of the parts
may become the rootstock of an orchard
and pathway to a thousand fields,
if these moments lead to....

4.

love and duty. Du Fu, when the gates
of harmony were smashed and the rebels advanced,
he had to decide, Emperor or family
and the only route to life led through fields
where rats and dogs fed on soldiers' flesh
where the paths through mountains were dissolving
when his shoes wore out
and the mud gripped his naked legs
and ice filled his nostrils
when his food was exhausted and only
the kindness of strangers, albeit tea and gruel,
replenished him; until he left behind the snow,
the sight of rebel armies
all this time, these miles
never knowing if or who he would find;
when at last he staggered into the village;
there duty and love, bound by rags and hope
came together.

5.

The bridge floats unmoored
as fog conceals the river
and another pledge is made
in brass and steel.
Immeasurable future,
mortality reserved for other people.

6.

Headlock: one hand alone
controls the key, the other turns
the cider-press screw,
fingers juiced in acid, flight
imagined through a crack in a wall...

7.

Art or engineering, the construction
of a bridge? Span, foundations,
arms outstretched to locate
the perfect centre
for opposing congruent weight and will
the point precise enough
to place the keystone
then to stand above and watch
the silvered flow, drop sticks,
dawdle, plan, look back. Intention
and fulfilment,
the mysteries of love.

                                         /continued

8.

The lovers have departed.
Mist beads the padlocks
while we stand trying to remember
the path which led us here.
Can love be such a burden?

Love will bear its weight
and much, much more.
The starting point is known
the end is always moving,
and in between, unpredictable weathers,
flowers in every season.

Love is love is love is love…

Well, obviously, as vole is vole and window window.
The logic is unbreakable but it's still
a noun mired in its circularity,
a serpent nibbling its tail
locked into its own Socratic debate.

Just open the bloody door marked "transitive verb"
and venture into
feeding at 4am through aching nipples,
cleaning the incontinent sphincter,
on hunger strike for the captive wife,
love, all the time persisting, persisting
knackered, yes but still persisting.

Study the bleak region where no offer is ever made,
abandoned orphans in shit-smeared cots.
Wander discreetly the rooms of offer and rejection
where love and hope have been confounded.

Sit in the public theatre
where love of self, first and always first,
is a black hole of voracious space
and dying time.

Loving is love compounding
with blood and air and water
driving the heart-beat of the cosmos.

Du Fu Comes to Our Home

Slowly, darkness cloaks our garden.
A light approaches, a man and his family

drag themselves towards our home. I bow.
We offer food, drink, beds, fresh clothes. Later,

He and i sit and share a pitcher of wine. Owls call,
we glimpse wide-winged moths. I listen.

"The rivers churned with bitter water, salt invaded
 fields; children fought in squalid pools for snails;

corpses rode in the ochre current; who noticed?
Families salvaged timber from the river, hovels collapsed.

On hillsides beyond an impregnable fence
rice danced in the golden light; melting pears

glutted the air; fire-red apples fell unpicked. Warlords prowled,
sought enemies though we worked quietly,

making paper and dyeing cloth. Who grafted the poison-tree
on the rootstock of the healthy rose, who grinds its leaves

to taint our drink?" He holds his breath;
he is rising from a deep pool.

"War destroyed our home, tracked our footsteps,
no sanctuary was safe. Fear woke us every morning.

We escaped down long rivers of tears. How can a man
plant an orchard if he has to flee, how find

a school for children's tranquil learning, how serve
the Emperor when the gates are broken down?"

A long shriek startles, air bristles with the scent of blood.
Stars jostle in the crystal sky.

"Stranger, friend, your words have travelled centuries
over mountains, along deep valleys. You are revered,

cartographer of beauty and disaster, whereas I watch our world
through shuttered windows, rattle words like sticks

in an empty yard. You have walked beyond endurance.
There is no need to journey further.
We offer you welcome and asylum.

We have a field where you and I might plant an orchard.
Perhaps
one day you may help me sow and harvest words."

Frank McMahon– Biography

Frank McMahon was born and raised in Birkenhead, Merseyside. After graduating he began his career in Social Work/ Welfare as a practitioner and manager, working for three Local Authorities, British Red Cross and ActionforChildren. He also served for nine years as a school governor. He is married with two children and six grandchildren. In January 2020 Palewell Press published his first volume of poems, "At the Storm's Edge."

When not writing (plays, a novel, short stories and poems) he enjoys walking – The Cotswolds are his new playground; his allotment, travel, music, and counts himself fortunate to have some wonderful friendships. He is a member of Somewhere Else Writers and Wordbrew Groups in Cirencester, whom he thanks for their patience in reading and critiquing his work. In 2021 he read at the Cheltenham Poetry Festival.

Palewell Press

Palewell Press is an independent publisher handling poetry, fiction and non-fiction with a focus on books that foster Justice, Equality and Sustainability. The Editor can be reached on enquiries@palewellpress.co.uk

www.ingramcontent.com/pod-product-compliance
Lightning Source LLC
Chambersburg PA
CBHW071124030426
42336CB00013BA/2196